BOOST™
SERIOUSLY *fun* LEARNING

GRADES 3 TO 5

ALIGNS TO THE **COMMON CORE STATE STANDARDS**

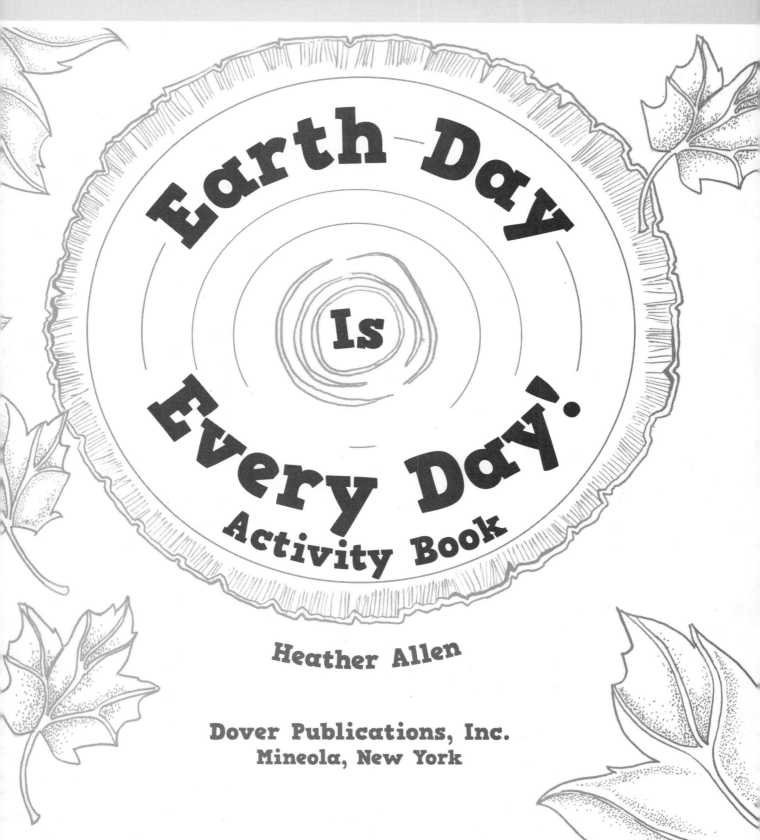

Earth Day Is Every Day!
Activity Book

Heather Allen

Dover Publications, Inc.
Mineola, New York

Bibliographical Note

BOOST Earth Day Is Every Day! Activity Book, first printed by Dover
Publications, Inc., in 2013, is a revised edition of *Earth Day Is Every Day!,*
originally published by Dover in 2011.

International Standard Book Number
ISBN-13: 978-0-486-49433-3
ISBN-10: 0-486-49433-0

Manufactured in the United States by Courier Corporation
49433001   2013
www.doverpublications.com

Introducing...

TEAM RECYCLE!

Dan

Helen

Joshua

Ashanti

Charlie

Meet the members of *Team Recycle!* You're invited to go with them on a special trip through the pages of this book, where they'll tell you all about the different ways we can help make the Earth a cleaner, healthier place to live.

As you complete mazes, number codes, crossword puzzles, hidden pictures, and other fun puzzles and activities, you'll learn about pollution and other environmental facts, plus the different ways in which you can help save planet Earth! Try to complete all the activities on your own, but if you get stuck, just turn to the Solutions section, beginning on page 36.

Let's get started!

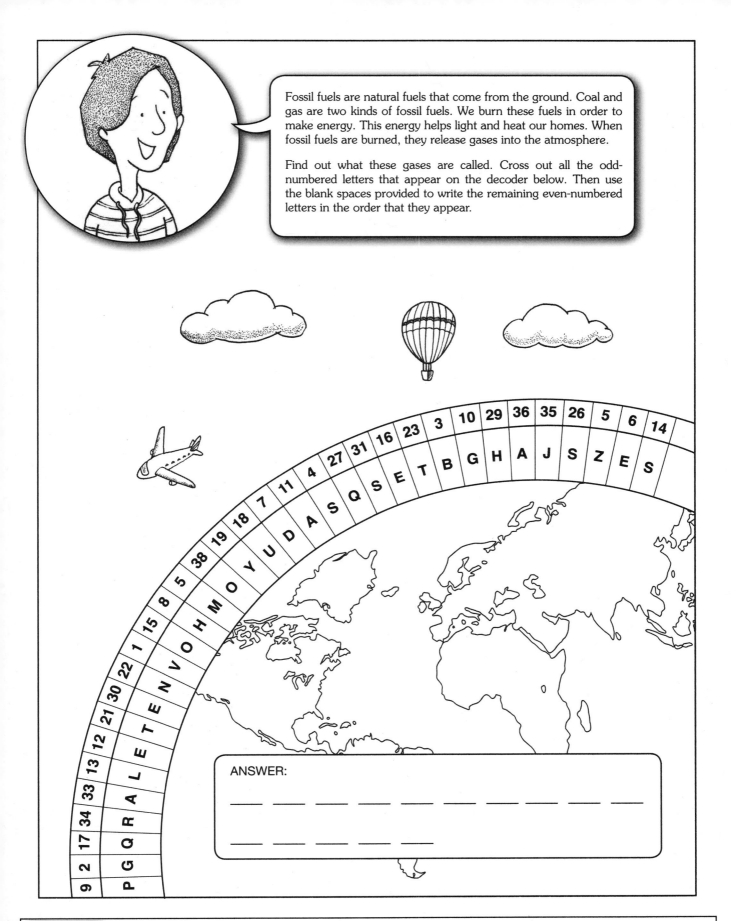

Fossil fuels are natural fuels that come from the ground. Coal and gas are two kinds of fossil fuels. We burn these fuels in order to make energy. This energy helps light and heat our homes. When fossil fuels are burned, they release gases into the atmosphere.

Find out what these gases are called. Cross out all the odd-numbered letters that appear on the decoder below. Then use the blank spaces provided to write the remaining even-numbered letters in the order that they appear.

ANSWER:

___ ___ ___ ___ ___ ___ ___

___ ___ ___ ___ ___ ___

CCSS RI.3.2 Determine the main idea of a text; recount the key details and explain how they support the main idea. Also **RI.3.1, L.3.6; RI.4.1, RI.4.2, L.4.6; RI.5.1, RI.5.2, L.5.6.**

1

Greenhouse gases float high in the atmosphere. They trap heat from the sun. This helps keep our planet warm. Without greenhouse gases, Earth would be too cold. However, *too many* greenhouse gases are harmful to the planet because they make the Earth *too* warm.

Complete the crossword puzzle below by writing the name of each picture in the spaces next to it. The circled letters, once unscrambled, will reveal the phrase used to describe the warming of Earth's air and oceans.

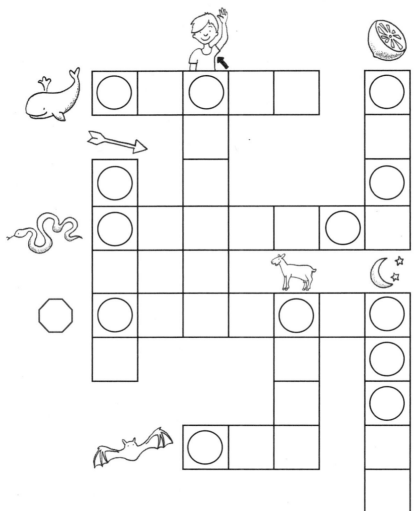

LETTERS: ___ ___ ___ ___ ___ ___ ___ ___ ___ ___ ___ ___ ___

UNSCRAMBLED
ANSWER: ___ ___ ___ ___ ___ ___ ___ ___ ___ ___ ___ ___ ___

CCSS **RI.3.4** Determine the meaning of general academic and domain-specific words and phrases in a text relevant to a *grade 3 topic or subject area*. Also **RI.3.2, RF.3.4.a; RI.4.2, RI.4.4, RF.4.4.a; RI.5.2, RI.5.4, RF.5.4.a.**

The trash we send to the garbage dump produces a very strong, harmful, greenhouse gas. Find and circle the seven hidden letters in the dump below. Unscramble them to find out the name of this gas.

LETTERS: ___ ___ ___ ___ ___ ___ ___

UNSCRAMBLED ANSWER: ___ ___ ___ ___ ___ ___ ___

CCSS **RI.3.1** Ask and answer questions to demonstrate understanding of a text, referring explicitly to the text as the basis for the answers. Also **RI.3.7, SL.3.1; RI.4.1, RI.4.7, SL.4.1; RI.5.1, SL.5.1.**

Can you find these?

1 banana peel	1 apple core	1 newspaper
1 milk bottle	1 paper airplane	1 milk carton
1 plastic bottle	pile of leaves	2 soda cans
vegetable peelings	2 cardboard boxes	5 paper cups
1 aluminum food can	pile of magazines	

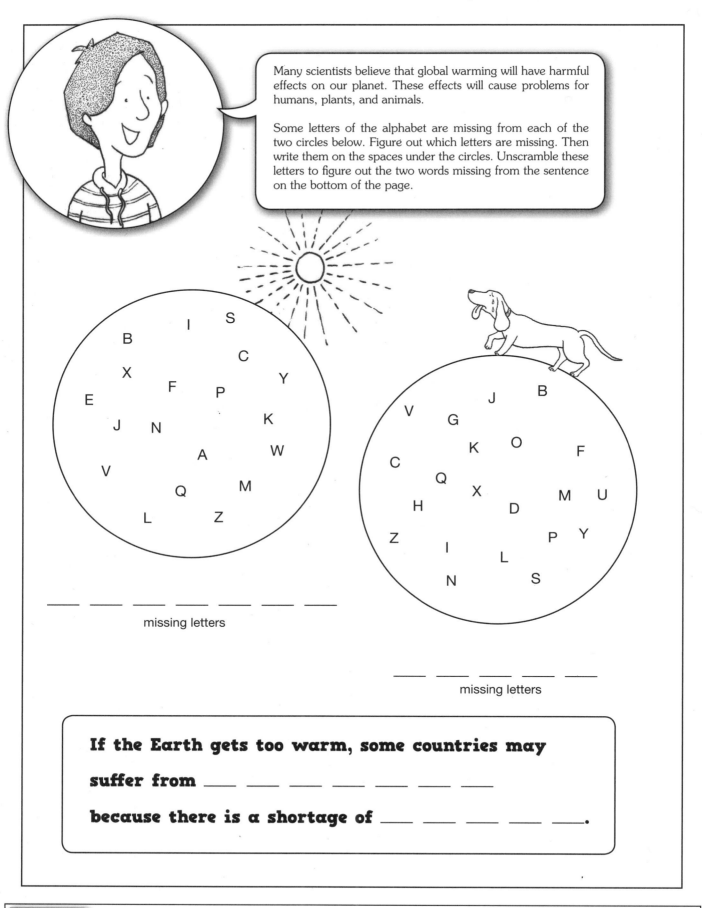

Many scientists believe that global warming will have harmful *effects* on our planet. These effects will cause problems for humans, plants, and animals.

Some letters of the alphabet are missing from each of the two circles below. Figure out which letters are missing. Then write them on the spaces under the circles. Unscramble these letters to figure out the two words missing from the sentence on the bottom of the page.

B I S
X C Y
E F P
J N K
A W
V Q M
L Z

___ ___ ___ ___ ___ ___

missing letters

V J B
G K O F
C Q X M U
H D
Z I P Y
N L S

___ ___ ___ ___

missing letters

If the Earth gets too warm, some countries may

suffer from ___ ___ ___ ___ ___ ___

because there is a shortage of ___ ___ ___ ___ ___.

CCSS **RI.3.1** Ask and answer questions to demonstrate understanding of a text, referring explicitly to the text as the basis for the answers. Also **RI.3.10; RI.4.1, RI.4.10; RI.5.1, RI.5.10.**

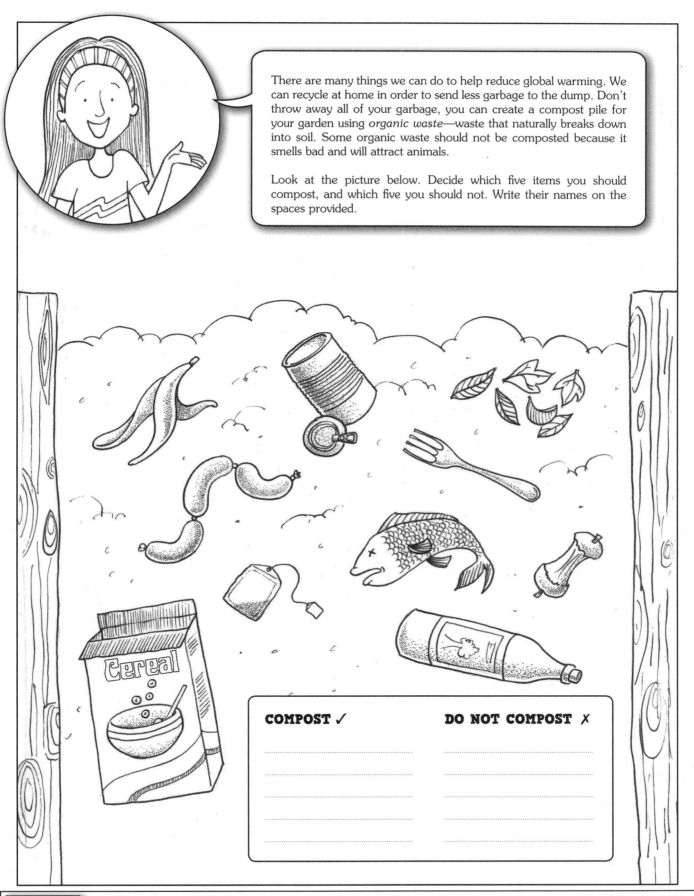

There are many things we can do to help reduce global warming. We can recycle at home in order to send less garbage to the dump. Don't throw away all of your garbage, you can create a compost pile for your garden using *organic waste*—waste that naturally breaks down into soil. Some organic waste should not be composted because it smells bad and will attract animals.

Look at the picture below. Decide which five items you should compost, and which five you should not. Write their names on the spaces provided.

COMPOST ✓

....

....

....

....

....

DO NOT COMPOST ✗

....

....

....

....

....

CCSS RI.3.3 Describe the relationship between a series of historical events, scientific ideas or concepts, or steps in technical procedures in a text, using language that pertains to time, sequence, and cause/effect. Also **RI.3.1, L.3.6; RI.4.1, RI.4.3, L.4.6; RI.5.1, RI.5.3, L.5.6.**

Trees are important because they clean the air by breathing in a harmful greenhouse gas and breathing out oxygen.

Circle all the letters in the decoder that are below a flower. Write these letters in the spaces provided to complete the sentence and find out which gas trees breathe in.

◆	✿	♥	✶	◆	♥	✿	✶	✿	✶
X	C	A	P	W	O	A	E	R	X
♥	✶	◆	✿	♥	✶	◆	✿	♥	✿
P	Y	H	B	R	S	G	O	T	N
✿	♥	✶	♥	✿	◆	♥	✿	✶	♥
D	M	H	Q	I	R	E	O	I	O
✶	✿	◆	✿	✶	◆	✿	◆	♥	✿
I	X	T	I	N	O	O	D	B	E

Trees breathe in...

__ __ __ __ __ __ __   __ __ __ __ __ __

...and breathe out oxygen.

CCSS **RI.3.2** Determine the main idea of a text; recount the key details and explain how they support the main idea. Also **RI.3.1, L.3.4.d; RI.4.1, RI.4.2, L.4.4.c; RI.5.1, L.5.4.c.**

You can conserve water at home by turning off the tap while brushing your teeth. Even a small action like this can make a difference to the environment. The Earth has only a limited supply of fresh water, so we need to use it wisely. Imagine if rivers, lakes, and wells dried up. Humans, plants, and animals would all suffer.

Look at the two pictures below. Circle ten things in the picture on the right that make it different from the one on the left.

 RI.3.9 Compare and contrast the most important points and key details presented in two texts on the same topic. Also **RI.3.3, RI.3.7, SL.3.1; RI.4.3, RI.4.7, RI.4.9, SL.4.1; RI.5.3, SL.5.1.**

Clearing the land of forests by chopping down or burning trees is called *deforestation*. The rainforest is home to many animals, and if too many trees are chopped down they will have nowhere to live. This can cause them to become endangered or even extinct.

Unscramble the words in the box. Write them on the blanks provided to learn the names of six animals that are currently losing their homes to deforestation. Then study the picture below. Find and circle each of the six animals.

NATCOU	RAGLOLI	GAJAUR
TOGRUNAAN	LAGEE	AWACM
_____	_____	_____
_____	_____	_____

RI.3.4 Determine the meaning of general academic and domain-specific words and phrases in a text relevant to a *grade 3 topic or subject area.* Also **RI.3.1, RF.3.4; RI.4.1, RI.4.4, RF.4.4; RI.5.1, RI.5.4, RF.5.4.**

When we burn fossil fuels to make things like gasoline, we are creating carbon dioxide, a harmful greenhouse gas. An alternative to burning fossil fuels is to use renewable fuels from plants and animals. For example, we can use the oils from plants or cow manure to create energy. This type of fuel is called *biofuel*.

How many times can you find the word **biofuel** in the grid below? You can move backward, forward, up, down, or across the grid, but never diagonally. The first one is done for you.

B	E	L	B	I	B	L
I	U	O	L	L	I	L
F	F	I	E	E	O	L
U	O	F	U	U	F	E
E	I	I	F	B	O	U
L	B	B	O	B	O	F
B	I	O	I	B	I	O

CCSS RI.3.2 Determine the main idea of a text; recount the key details and explain how they support the main idea. Also **RI.3.1, L.3.4.d; RI.4.1, RI.4.2, L.4.4.c; RI.5.1, RI.5.2, L.5.4.c.**

The Earth is surrounded by a layer of gases that protects the planet from the harmful rays of the sun.

Find out what this layer is called by solving the picture puzzle below. Write the name of each animal on the space next to it, and then unscramble the letters in the box to get the answer.

LETTERS: __ __ __ __ __ __ __

UNSCRAMBLED ANSWER: __ __ __ __ __ __ __ __ __ __ __ __ __

Look at the cards below. They show some ways to reduce global warming and save energy.

Cut out the cards. Turn all of them over so that the Save Energy! side is face up. Mix the cards. Two or more players can take turns flipping them over two at a time. If you find a matching pair, keep it. Then take another turn. If your pair doesn't match, turn the cards back face down. The next player takes a turn. The winner is the player with the most matching pairs at the end of the game.

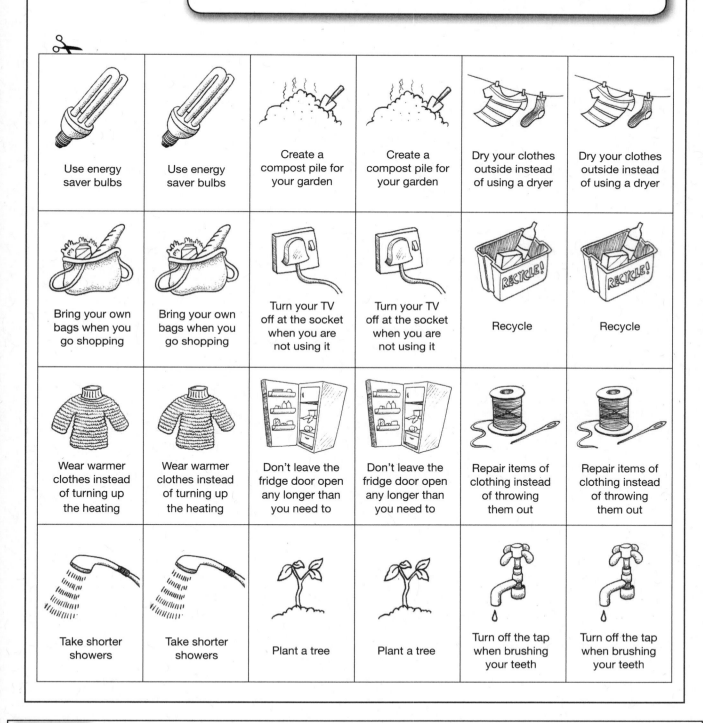

Use energy saver bulbs	Use energy saver bulbs	Create a compost pile for your garden	Create a compost pile for your garden	Dry your clothes outside instead of using a dryer	Dry your clothes outside instead of using a dryer
Bring your own bags when you go shopping	Bring your own bags when you go shopping	Turn your TV off at the socket when you are not using it	Turn your TV off at the socket when you are not using it	Recycle	Recycle
Wear warmer clothes instead of turning up the heating	Wear warmer clothes instead of turning up the heating	Don't leave the fridge door open any longer than you need to	Don't leave the fridge door open any longer than you need to	Repair items of clothing instead of throwing them out	Repair items of clothing instead of throwing them out
Take shorter showers	Take shorter showers	Plant a tree	Plant a tree	Turn off the tap when brushing your teeth	Turn off the tap when brushing your teeth

CCSS **RI.3.7** Use information gained from illustrations and the words in a text to demonstrate understanding of the text. Also **RI.3.1, SL.3.1.a; RI.4.1, RI.4.7, SL.4.1.a; RI.5.1, SL.5.1.a.**

Can you think of any other ways to help the environment?
Use construction paper to make your own matching-pairs game!

Save Energy!	Save Energy!	Save Energy!	Save Energy!	Save Energy!	Save Energy!
Save Energy!	Save Energy!	Save Energy!	Save Energy!	Save Energy!	Save Energy!
Save Energy!	Save Energy!	Save Energy!	Save Energy!	Save Energy!	Save Energy!
Save Energy!	Save Energy!	Save Energy!	Save Energy!	Save Energy!	Save Energy!

 RI.3.6 Distinguish their own point of view from that of the author of a text. Also **RI.3.10**; **RI.4.3, RI.4.10; RI.5.10.**

Find the ecological words listed in the box at the bottom of the page in the word search.

L	K	B	L	I	A	L	R	G	A	E	U	P	H	C	I
I	G	H	K	N	L	Q	K	U	L	S	D	E	G	K	U
U	L	G	G	U	U	T	H	C	U	T	N	X	T	Y	D
M	I	Q	R	C	M	D	Y	I	M	P	R	T	S	G	Q
G	N	X	N	E	N	C	B	P	I	D	E	U	R	R	S
D	E	S	K	Q	E	S	D	R	N	I	N	I	M	E	H
G	E	N	E	R	I	N	Q	E	U	T	E	U	H	N	I
C	R	L	K	T	P	X	H	U	M	K	W	R	R	E	U
H	R	A	I	S	O	L	K	O	M	I	A	G	D	K	N
U	A	R	N	B	C	E	H	C	U	R	B	Y	X	G	D
S	L	S	H	N	X	U	I	O	Q	S	L	U	H	R	N
T	O	T	C	T	S	D	P	R	T	P	E	Q	C	E	Q
K	S	N	I	Q	E	E	N	G	C	I	N	A	G	R	O
N	D	N	P	R	H	S	B	A	C	R	O	U	S	E	S
G	C	K	C	T	I	U	D	X	P	S	U	P	D	X	U
T	I	S	P	C	T	U	R	B	I	N	E	N	G	H	N

GREENHOUSE	ORGANIC	ENERGY
RENEWABLE	ALUMINUM	TURBINE
RECYCLE	EXTINCT	SOLAR

CCSS **RI.3.4** Determine the meaning of general academic and domain-specific words and phrases in a text relevant to a *grade 3 topic or subject area.* Also **RI.3.1, RI.3.7; RI.4.1, RI.4.4, RI.4.7; RI.5.4.**

Newspapers can be recycled. So can plastic bottles and aluminum cans. Trace a path from each of these objects through the maze to the recycling bin in the center.

RECYCLE!

If you look at the stump of a tree that has been cut down, you can see many rings inside it. These rings grow over many years. They give us an idea of the tree's age.

Scientists can tell a lot about past climates by studying tree rings. If the ring is narrow, that means the tree did not grow very much, and it is likely that there wasn't much rain that year. If the ring is wider, the tree grew a lot. It is probable that spring came early. The advantage of using trees to study climate is that they are living records of past weather patterns. They may help us to be more prepared for global warming in the future.

To find out what we call the study of tree rings, cross out the letters that appear *four* times in the tree ring grid. Then list the remaining letters on the blank spaces provided.

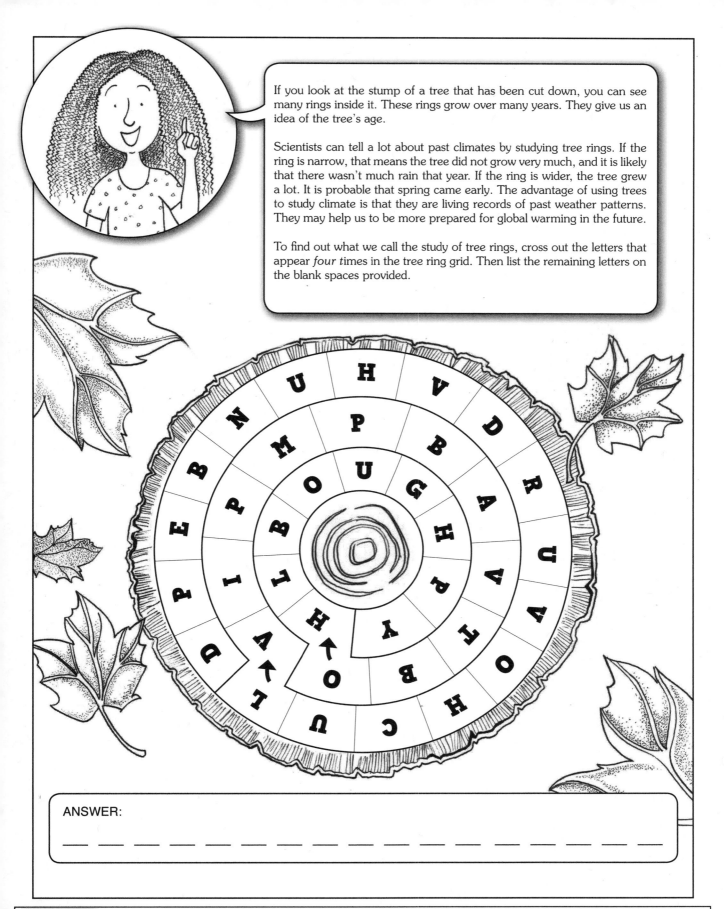

ANSWER:

___ ___ ___ ___ ___ ___ ___ ___ ___ ___ ___

CCSS **RI.3.3** Describe the relationship between a series of historical events, scientific ideas or concepts, or steps in technical procedures in a text, using language that pertains to time, sequence, and cause/effect. Also **RI.3.1, RI.3.4, SL.3.1; RI.4.1, RI.4.3, RI.4.4, SL.4.1; RI.5.1, RI.5.3, RI.5.4, SL.5.1.**

 CCSS **RI.3.7** Use information gained from illustrations and the words in a text to demonstrate understanding of the text. Also **RI.3.4, RI.3.10; RI.4.4, RI.4.7, RI.4.10; RI.5.4, RI.5.10.**

Plants make food for themselves through a chemical process that uses energy from the sun. They soak up sunlight through their leaves and turn it into food in the form of glucose.

Find out the word used to describe this important process. Write the letters on the leaves in number order (1–14) on the blank spaces provided.

ANSWER:

_____ _____ _____ _____ _____ _____ _____ _____ _____ _____ _____ _____ _____ _____

It's not just manmade activities that produce harmful greenhouse gases. Animal waste produces methane just like a garbage dump does. One animal in particular produces a lot of this gas—cows!

Reveal the cow hidden in the puzzle below by shading the right areas.

CCSS **RI.3.2** Determine the main idea of a text; recount the key details and explain how they support the main idea. Also **RI.3.1, SL.3.1.a, L.3.4.d; RI.4.1, RI.4.2, SL.4.1.a, L.4.4.c; RI.5.1, RI.5.2, SL.5.1.a, L.5.4.c.**

Earth Day was founded in 1970 by a U.S. senator who wanted to make the world more aware of pollution and the effect it was having on our environment. He organized rallies all over the United States. People joined in to speak out against many environmental issues, including oil spills, factory pollution, raw sewage, toxic dumps, and the extinction of wildlife.

To find out the name of this senator, answer each clue below on the blank spaces provided. The circled letters, written in the order that they appear, will spell out his name.

Waste we throw in a bin ⊝ — — ⊝ — —

Trees produce this gas — — ⊝ — — —

This might happen to low-lying land if sea levels rise — ⊝ — ⊝ — —

Plant one of these to help the environment — ⊝ — —

A form of renewable energy — — — ⊝

Garbage dumps produce this gas — — — — — ⊝⊝

Bottles are made from this and it can be recycled — ⊝ — ⊝ —

The protective layer around the Earth ⊝ — — ⊝ — —

ANSWER:

__ __ __ __ __ __ __ __   __ __ __ __ __ __ __ __

 RI.3.3 Describe the relationship between a series of historical events, scientific ideas or concepts, or steps in technical procedures in a text, using language that pertains to time, sequence, and cause/effect. Also **RI.3.1, L.3.4; RI.4.1, RI.4.3, L.4.4; RI.5.1, RI.5.3, L.5.4.**

21

The more we use cars, the more fossil fuels we need to burn in order to make the gasoline that runs them. Exhaust fumes also pollute the air. They are unhealthy to breathe in.

What can you do to reduce air pollution?

Use this chart to decode the answer.

A	B	C	D	E	F	I	K
3	13	6	14	8	5	4	16
L	**N**	**O**	**R**	**S**	**T**	**V**	**W**
11	1	15	9	2	7	12	10

___ ___ ___ ___   ___   ___ ___ ___ ___   ___ ___
9   4   14   8   3   13   4   16   8   15   9

___ ___ ___ ___   ___ ___ ___ ___ ___ ___ ___
10   3   11   16   4   1   2   7   8   3   14

___ ___   ___ ___ ___ ___ ___
15   5   14   9   4   12   8

CCSS RI.3.2 Determine the main idea of a text; recount the key details and explain how they support the main idea. Also **RI.3.4, RI.3.7, SL.3.1.a; RI.4.2, RI.4.4, RI.4.7, SL.4.1.a; RI.5.2, RI.5.4, SL.5.1.a.**

Answer the ecological clues to complete the crossword puzzle.

Across
1 This footprint you cannot see, but it can be measured and reduced to help preserve the environment
4 Help protect this by using less energy and reducing pollution
5 Turn these off around the house when you don't need them, so you can save energy
7 Trees produce this gas
8 Instead of throwing food waste in the garbage, you can recycle it in the garden with this

Down
2 This helps to protect our planet from the sun's harmful rays
3 Doing this will reduce the amount of rubbish sent to landfills
6 A very large area that is threatened by deforestation and is the home of many animals
9 Type of waste that will break down easily into the soil

 RI.3.1 Ask and answer questions to demonstrate understanding of a text, referring explicitly to the text as the basis for the answers. Also **RI.3.10; RI.4.1, RI.4.10; RI.5.1, RI.5.10.**

Not all garbage takes the same amount of time to break down. Follow the path from each piece of trash to find out how long each one takes to decompose. Then write the name of each object in the correct column in the chart.

500 years	6 months
....	....
....	....

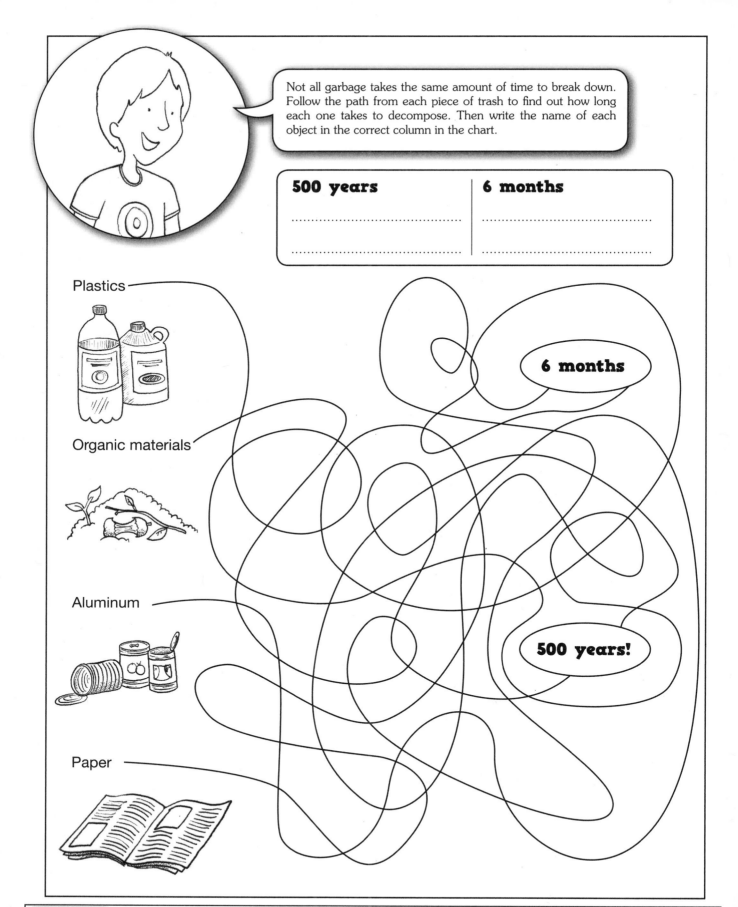

Plastics

Organic materials

Aluminum

Paper

6 months

500 years!

CCSS **RI.3.4** Determine the meaning of general academic and domain-specific words and phrases in a text relevant to a *grade 3 topic or subject area.* Also **RI.3.2, SL.3.1; RI.4.2, RI.4.4, SL.4.1; RI.5.2, RI.5.4, SL.5.1.**

There is about 25% more carbon dioxide in the air today than there was in 1860. Cutting down and burning trees is one of the biggest sources of carbon dioxide.

How can you reduce the amount of carbon dioxide in the air? Connect the dots to find out.

Did you know that turning on a light switch in your home produces greenhouse gases? If the electricity in your home comes from a power plant, then the plant has to burn fossil fuels to create electricity. Burning fossil fuels produces the greenhouse gas carbon dioxide. Remember to turn off the lights when you don't really need them on!

Leaving a 60W bulb on overnight when not needed consumes enough energy to make _____ cups of tea.

$32 - (48 \div 8) - 2$

A 100W regular light bulb left on for just _____ minutes creates enough CO_2 to fill a party balloon.

$(3 \times 6 \times 2) - (28 + 2)$

An energy-saving light bulb uses approximately _____ % of the energy consumed by a normal light bulb.

5^2

An energy-saving light bulb lasts _____ times longer than a regular bulb.

$(24 \div 6) \times 5 - 10$

One large office lit overnight wastes enough energy to drive a small car more than _____ miles.

$1800 \div 9$

CCSS **RI.3.3** Describe the relationship between a series of historical events, scientific ideas or concepts, or steps in technical procedures in a text, using language that pertains to time, sequence, and cause/effect. Also **RI.3.1, L.3.6; RI.4.1, RI.4.3, L.4.6; RI.5.1, RI.5.3, L.5.6.**

Renewable energy does not create greenhouse gases. It comes from natural resources like water, sun, and wind. Only 7% of the world's energy is created from renewable resources. Renewable energy may become more common in the future.

Wind power is one form of renewable energy. Big turbines turn in the wind, and the energy this creates is turned into electricity.

Rearrange the letters in the puzzle to reveal an amazing fact about renewable energy. When completed, the grid can be read from left to right. Each blank space needs to be filled in with a letter. This will create a word in each group of spaces. Each space must be filled in with one letter from the column above it. The word **wind** and the number **300** have been done for you to get you started. Each letter can only be used once, so cross it out after you have used it. Use a pencil for this activity, since it might take you a few tries to get it right!

Columns

1	2	3	4	5	6	7	8	9
C	A	E		H	O	N̶		
3̶	0̶	R		W̶	N	W	E	
O	N	0̶		P	O	E	D̶	S
T	U	N	B	I	I̶	M	E	R
				W	**I**	**N**	**D**	
3	**0**	**0**						

CCSS **RI.3.2** Determine the main idea of a text; recount the key details and explain how they support the main idea. Also **RI.3.4, RI.3.10; RI.4.2, RI.4.4, RI.4.10; RI.5.2, RI.5.4, RI.5.10.**

Our *carbon footprint* is the amount of greenhouse gas we produce every day. The more carbon dioxide we release into the atmosphere, the bigger our footprint.

Cars burn gasoline to make them work, releasing lots of carbon dioxide into the air. The more we use cars, the bigger our carbon footprint. You can reduce your carbon footprint by carpooling, taking public transportation, riding a bicycle, or walking.

Complete the puzzle below by drawing the four types of transportation symbols on the grid. Each horizontal and vertical row must contain "bus," "cycle," "carpool," and "walk." Each symbol can appear only once in each row.

Transportation symbols

bus

cycle

carpool

walk

RI.3.4 Determine the meaning of general academic and domain-specific words and phrases in a text relevant to a *grade 3 topic or subject area.* Also **RI.3.1, RF.3.4.a, L.3.6; RI.4.1, RI.4.4, RF.4.4.a, L.4.6; RI.5.1, RI.5.4, RF.5.4.a, L.5.6.**

Water covers 70% of the Earth's surface. If global warming makes the sea level rise, the water could flood the land. People, animals, and plants would lose their homes.

Scientists divide the Earth's main body of water into four oceans. Unscramble the name of each ocean. Write it on the blank spaces provided.

CATRIC

— — — — — —

LIANTACT

— — — — — — — —

NADIIN

— — — — —

FACIPCI

— — — — — — —

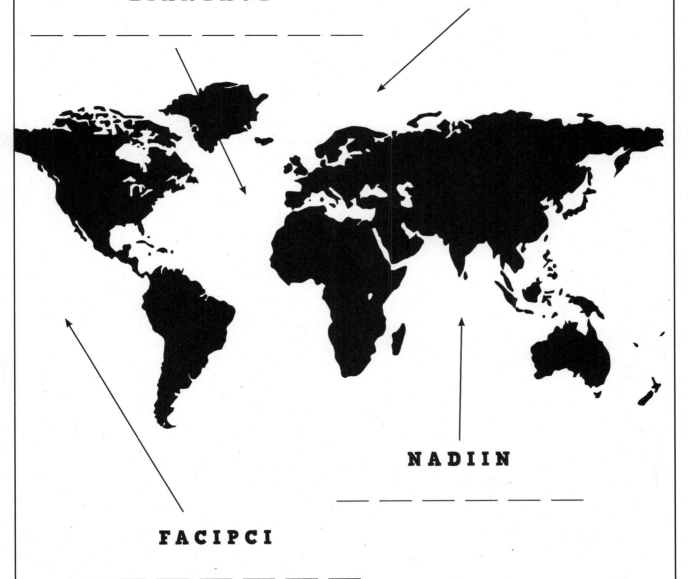

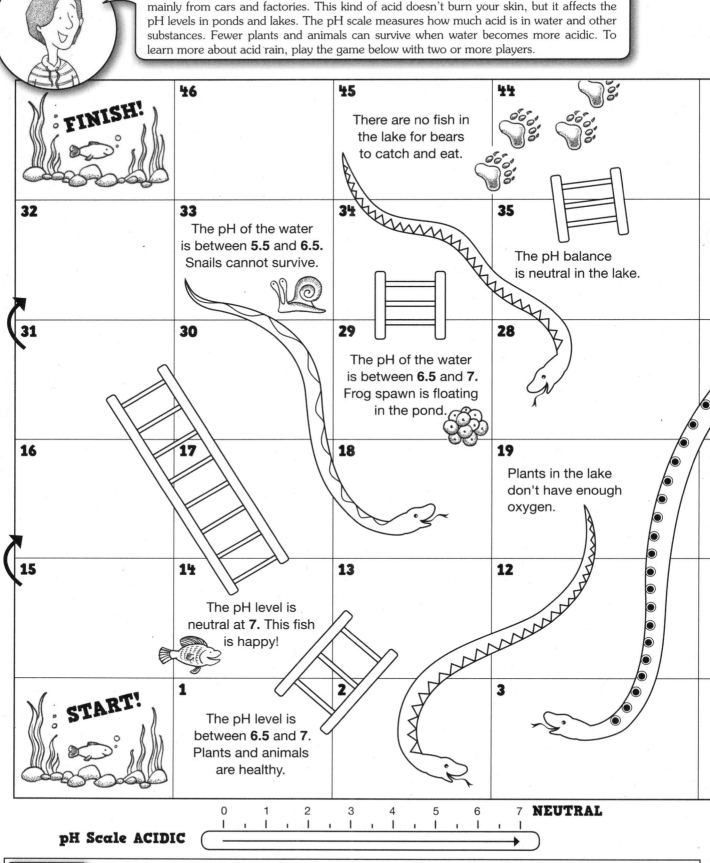

Acid rain occurs when certain chemicals mix with pollution in the air. The pollution comes mainly from cars and factories. This kind of acid doesn't burn your skin, but it affects the pH levels in ponds and lakes. The pH scale measures how much acid is in water and other substances. Fewer plants and animals can survive when water becomes more acidic. To learn more about acid rain, play the game below with two or more players.

FINISH!

46

45 — There are no fish in the lake for bears to catch and eat.

44

32

33 — The pH of the water is between **5.5** and **6.5**. Snails cannot survive.

34

35 — The pH balance is neutral in the lake.

31

30

29 — The pH of the water is between **6.5** and **7**. Frog spawn is floating in the pond.

28

16

17

18

19 — Plants in the lake don't have enough oxygen.

15

14 — The pH level is neutral at **7**. This fish is happy!

13

12

START!

1 — The pH level is between **6.5** and **7**. Plants and animals are healthy.

2

3

0 1 2 3 4 5 6 7 **NEUTRAL**

pH Scale ACIDIC

CCSS RI.3.3 Describe the relationship between a series of historical events, scientific ideas or concepts, or steps in technical procedures in a text, using language that pertains to time, sequence, and cause/effect. Also **RI.3.4, RI.3.7, SL.3.1; RI.4.3, RI.4.4, RI.4.7, SL.4.1; RI.5.3, RI.5.4, SL.5.1.**

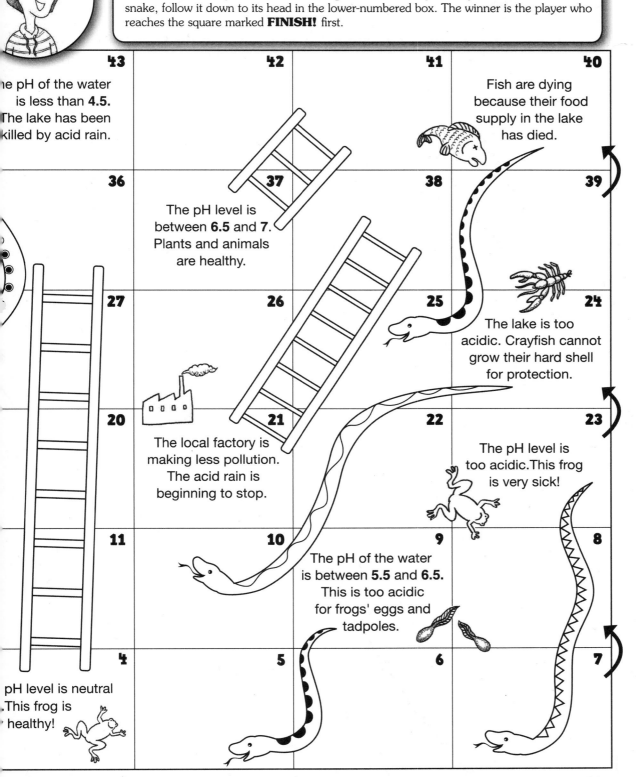

43 The pH of the water is less than **4.5.** The lake has been killed by acid rain.

42

41

40 Fish are dying because their food supply in the lake has died.

36

37 The pH level is between **6.5** and **7.** Plants and animals are healthy.

38

39

27

26

25

24 The lake is too acidic. Crayfish cannot grow their hard shell for protection.

20

21 The local factory is making less pollution. The acid rain is beginning to stop.

22

23 The pH level is too acidic. This frog is very sick!

11

10

9 The pH of the water is between **5.5** and **6.5.** This is too acidic for frogs' eggs and tadpoles.

8

4 pH level is neutral. This frog is healthy!

5

6

7

If you don't have a die, write the numbers 1–6 on separate pieces of paper. Mix them up. Let your opponent pick a number out of your hand without looking. Don't forget to recycle the paper afterwards!

Team Recycle has a motto to help us remember to be good to the environment. Unscramble the letters on the sign to find out what it is.

CUREED

SEERU

CREYLEC

ANSWER:

___ ___ ___ ___ ___ ___ , ___ ___ ___ ___ , ___ ___ ___ ___ ___ ___ !

Test your knowledge!

Match the solutions A–I with the clues 1–9. After you have matched each solution with a clue, write the number of the clue in the magic square. If correct, each column, row, and diagonal will add up to 15.

A =	**B** =	**C** =
D =	**E** =	**F** =
G =	**H** =	**I** =

A Dendroclimatology	**D** The founder of Earth Day	**G** Methane
B Acid Rain	**E** Aluminum	**H** Ice Glaciers
C E-waste	**F** Fossil Fuels	**I** Carbon Dioxide

1) These may melt because of global warming
2) This is a term for electronic waste
3) Gaylord Nelson
4) Scientists study tree rings to find out about our climate. What term describes their job?
5) This form of waste takes 500 years to break down
6) Cars produce this greenhouse gas
7) Natural resources found in the ground which we burn to make energy
8) This gas is emitted from cows' waste
9) When chemicals mix with water in the air they can poison lakes and animals may die

RI.3.1 Ask and answer questions to demonstrate understanding of a text, referring explicitly to the text as the basis for the answers. Also **RI.3.7, RF.3.4.a; RI.4.1, RI.4.7, RF.4.4.a; RI.5.1, RF.5.4.a.**

SOLUTIONS

Page 1

Fossil fuels are natural fuels that come from the ground. Coal and gas are two kinds of fossil fuels. We burn these fuels in order to make energy. This energy helps light and heat our homes. When fossil fuels are burned, they release gases into the atmosphere.

Find out what these gases are called. Cross out all the odd-numbered letters that appear on the decoder below. Then use the blank spaces provided to write the remaining even-numbered letters in the order that they appear.

ANSWER: G R E E N H O U S E
G A S E S

Page 2

Greenhouse gases float high in the atmosphere. They trap heat from the sun. This helps keep our planet warm. Without greenhouse gases, Earth would be too cold. However, too many greenhouse gases are harmful to the planet because they make the Earth too warm.

Complete the crossword puzzle below by writing the name of each picture in the spaces next to it. The circled letters, once unscrambled, will reveal the phrase used to describe the warming of Earth's air and oceans.

LETTERS: W A L A M R L O G N I G B
UNSCRAMBLED ANSWER: G L O B A L   W A R M I N G

Page 3

The trash we send to the garbage dump produces a very strong, harmful, greenhouse gas. Find and circle the seven hidden letters in the dump below. Unscramble them to find out the name of this gas.

LETTERS: A N H E T M E
UNSCRAMBLED ANSWER: M E T H A N E

Let's recycle! Look at the list on the opposite page, and then find the items listed in the picture.

WASH YOUR HANDS

Can you find these?

1 banana peel	1 apple core	1 newspaper
1 milk bottle	1 paper airplane	1 milk carton
1 plastic bottle	pile of leaves	2 soda cans
vegetable peelings	2 cardboard boxes	5 paper cups
1 aluminum food can	pile of magazines	

Page 6

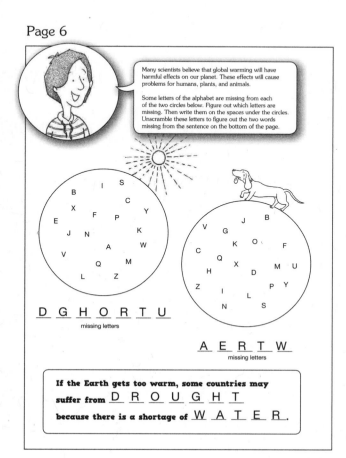

Many scientists believe that global warming will have harmful effects on our planet. These effects will cause problems for humans, plants, and animals.

Some letters of the alphabet are missing from each of the two circles below. Figure out which letters are missing. Then write them on the spaces under the circles. Unscramble these letters to figure out the two words missing from the sentence on the bottom of the page.

Circle 1 letters: B I S / X F P C Y / E J N A K W / V Q M / L Z

Circle 2 letters: V G J B / K O F / C Q X D MU / H / Z I L P Y / N S

D G H O R T U
missing letters

A E R T W
missing letters

If the Earth gets too warm, some countries may suffer from D R O U G H T because there is a shortage of W A T E R.

Page 7

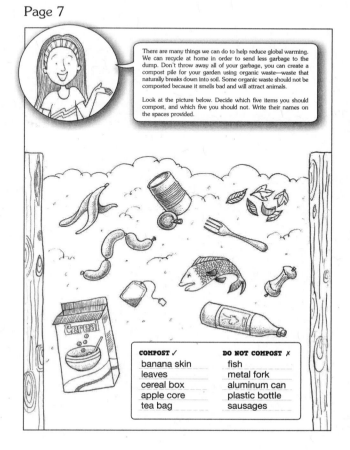

There are many things we can do to help reduce global warming. We can recycle at home in order to send less garbage to the dump. Don't throw away all of your garbage, you can create a compost pile for your garden using organic waste—waste that naturally breaks down into soil. Some organic waste should not be composted because it smells bad and will attract animals.

Look at the picture below. Decide which five items you should compost, and which five you should not. Write their names on the spaces provided.

Cereal

COMPOST ✓	DO NOT COMPOST ✗
banana skin	fish
leaves	metal fork
cereal box	aluminum can
apple core	plastic bottle
tea bag	sausages

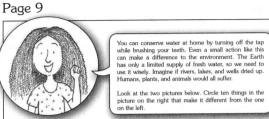

Trees are important because they clean the air by breathing in a harmful greenhouse gas and breathing out oxygen.

Circle all the letters in the decoder that are below a flower. Write these letters in the spaces provided to complete the sentence and find out which gas trees breathe in.

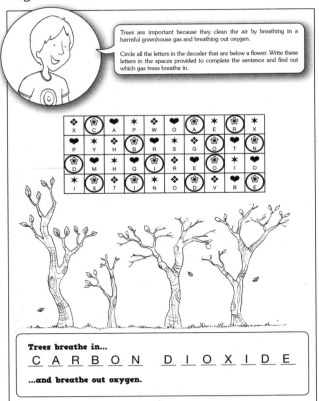

Trees breathe in...

C A R B O N   D I O X I D E

...and breathe out oxygen.

You can conserve water at home by turning off the tap while brushing your teeth. Even a small action like this can make a difference to the environment. The Earth has only a limited supply of fresh water, so we need to use it wisely. Imagine if rivers, lakes, and wells dried up. Humans, plants, and animals would all suffer.

Look at the two pictures below. Circle ten things in the picture on the right that make it different from the one on the left.

Clearing the land of forests by chopping down or burning trees is called *deforestation*. The rainforest is home to many animals, and if too many trees are chopped down they will have nowhere to live. This can cause them to become endangered or even extinct.

Unscramble the words in the box. Write them on the blanks provided to learn the names of six animals that are currently losing their homes to deforestation. Then study the picture below. Find and circle each of the six animals.

NATCOU	RAGLOLI	GAJAUR
TOGRUNAAN	LAGEE	AWACM
TOUCAN	**GORILLA**	**JAGUAR**
ORANGUTAN	**EAGLE**	**MACAW**

When we burn fossil fuels to make things like gasoline, we are creating carbon dioxide, a harmful greenhouse gas. An alternative to burning fossil fuels is to use renewable fuels from plants and animals. For example, we can use the oils from plants or cow manure to create energy. This type of fuel is called *biofuel*.

How many times can you find the word **biofuel** in the grid below? You can move backward, forward, up, down, or across the grid, but never diagonally. The first one is done for you.

Page 12

The Earth is surrounded by a layer of gases that protects the planet from the harmful rays of the sun.

Find out what this layer is called by solving the picture puzzle below. Write the name of each animal on the space next to it, and then unscramble the letters in the box to get the answer.

D O L P H I N
S H A R K
M O N K E Y
T I G E R
L I Z A R D
S H E E P
O C T O P U S
O X
E L E P H A N T
P A R R O T

LETTERS: L R Y E Z E O O N A

UNSCRAMBLED ANSWER: O Z O N E   L A Y E R

Page 15

Find the ecological words listed in the box at the bottom of the page in the word search.

L	K	B	L	I	A	L	R	G	A	E	U	P	H	C	I
I	G	H	K	N	L	Q	K	U	L	S	D	E	G	K	U
U	L	G	G	U	U	T	H	C	U	T	N	X	T	Y	D
N	I	Q	R	C	M	D	Y	I	M	P	R	T	S	G	Q
G	N	X	N	E	N	C	B	P	I	D	E	U	R	R	S
D	E	S	K	O	E	S	D	R	N	I	N	I	M	E	H
G	E	N	E	R	R	I	N	Q	E	U	T	E	U	H	N
C	R	L	K	T	P	X	H	U	M	K	W	R	R	E	I
H	R	A	I	S	O	L	K	O	M	I	A	G	D	K	N
U	A	R	N	B	C	E	H	C	U	R	B	Y	X	G	D
S	L	S	H	N	X	U	I	O	G	S	L	U	H	R	N
T	O	T	C	T	S	D	P	R	T	P	E	Q	C	E	Q
K	S	N	I	Q	E	E	N	G	C	I	N	A	G	R	O
N	D	N	P	R	H	S	B	A	C	R	O	U	S	E	S
G	C	K	C	T	I	U	D	X	P	S	U	P	D	X	U
T	I	S	P	C	T	U	R	B	I	N	E	N	G	H	N

GREENHOUSE	ORGANIC	ENERGY
RENEWABLE	ALUMINUM	TURBINE
RECYCLE	EXTINCT	SOLAR

Page 16

Newspapers can be recycled. So can plastic bottles and aluminum cans. Trace a path from each of these objects through the maze to the recycling bin in the center.

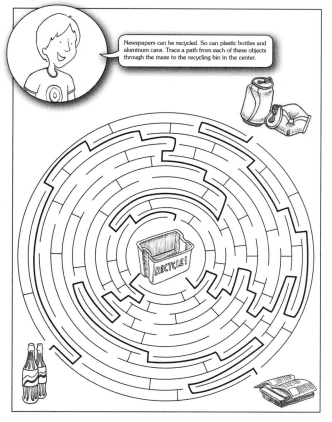

Page 17

If you look at the stump of a tree that has been cut down, you can see many rings inside it. These rings grow over many years. They give us an idea of the tree's age.

Scientists can tell a lot about past climates by studying tree rings. If the ring is narrow, that means the tree did not grow very much, and it is likely that there wasn't much rain that year. If the ring is wider, the tree grew a lot. It is probable that spring came early. The advantage of using trees to study climate is that they are living records of past weather patterns. They may help us to be more prepared for global warming in the future.

To find out what we call the study of tree rings, cross out the letters that appear four times in the tree ring grid. Then list the remaining letters on the blank spaces provided.

ANSWER:
D E N D R O C L I M A T O L O G Y

A good way to improve your local environment is to organize a cleanup. Litter makes your surroundings ugly. It can also harm animals if they mistake it for food.

Look at the picture below. Find and circle ten items of litter.

Plants make food for themselves through a chemical process that uses energy from the sun. They soak up sunlight through their leaves and turn it into food in the form of glucose.

Find out the word used to describe this important process. Write the letters on the leaves in number order (1–14) on the blank spaces provided.

ANSWER:
P H O T O S Y N T H E S I S

It's not just manmade activities that produce harmful greenhouse gases. Animal waste produces methane just like a garbage dump does. One animal in particular produces a lot of this gas—cows!

Reveal the cow hidden in the puzzle below by shading the right areas.

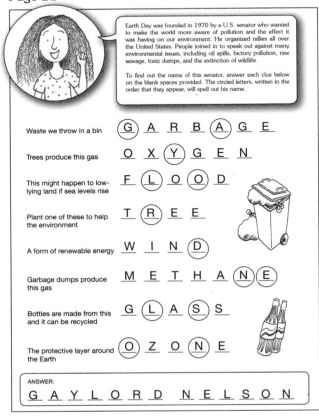

Earth Day was founded in 1970 by a U.S. senator who wanted to make the world more aware of pollution and the effect it was having on our environment. He organized rallies all over the United States. People joined in to speak out against many environmental issues, including oil spills, factory pollution, raw sewage, toxic dumps, and the extinction of wildlife.

To find out the name of this senator, answer each clue below on the blank spaces provided. The circled letters, written in the order that they appear, will spell out his name.

Waste we throw in a bin — G A R B A G E

Trees produce this gas — O X Y G E N

This might happen to low-lying land if sea levels rise — F L O O D

Plant one of these to help the environment — T R E E

A form of renewable energy — W I N D

Garbage dumps produce this gas — M E T H A N E

Bottles are made from this and it can be recycled — G L A S S

The protective layer around the Earth — O Z O N E

ANSWER:
G A Y L O R D   N E L S O N

The more we use cars, the more fossil fuels we need to burn in order to make the gasoline that runs them. Exhaust fumes also pollute the air. They are unhealthy to breathe in.

What can you do to reduce air pollution?

Use this chart to decode the answer.

A	B	C	D	E	F	I	K
3	13	6	14	8	4	16
L	N	O	R	S	T	V	W
11	1	15	9	2	7	12	10

R I D E   A   B I K E   O R
9 4 14 8   3   13 4 16 8   15 9

W A L K   I N S T E A D
10 3 11 16 4 1 2 7 8 3 14

O F   D R I V E .
15 5   14 9 4 12 8

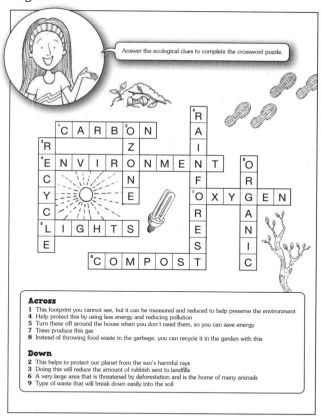

Answer the ecological clues to complete the crossword puzzle.

Crossword answers:
1 CARBON
2 OZONE
3 RECYCLE
4 ENVIRONMENT
5 LIGHTS
6 RAINFORESTS
7 OXYGEN
8 COMPOST
9 ORGANIC

Across
1 This footprint you cannot see, but it can be measured and reduced to help preserve the environment
4 Help protect this by using less energy and reducing pollution
5 Turn these off around the house when you don't need them, so you can save energy
7 Trees produce this gas
8 Instead of throwing food waste in the garbage, you can recycle it in the garden with this

Down
2 This helps to protect our planet from the sun's harmful rays
3 Doing this will reduce the amount of rubbish sent to landfills
6 A very large area that is threatened by deforestation and is the home of many animals
9 Type of waste that will break down easily into the soil

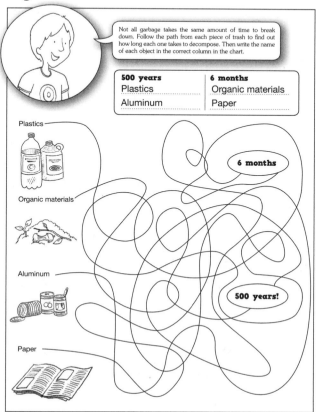

Not all garbage takes the same amount of time to break down. Follow the path from each piece of trash to find out how long each one takes to decompose. Then write the name of each object in the correct column in the chart.

500 years	6 months
Plastics	Organic materials
Aluminum	Paper

Plastics

Organic materials

Aluminum

Paper

6 months

500 years!

There is about 25% more carbon dioxide in the air today than there was in 1860. Cutting down and burning trees is one of the biggest sources of carbon dioxide.

How can you reduce the amount of carbon dioxide in the air? Connect the dots to find out.

Page 26

Did you know that turning on a light switch in your home produces greenhouse gases? If the electricity in your home comes from a power plant, then the plant has to burn fossil fuels to create electricity. Burning fossil fuels produces the greenhouse gas carbon dioxide. Remember to turn off the lights when you don't really need them on!

Leaving a 60W bulb on overnight when not needed consumes enough energy to make **24** cups of tea.

$32 - (48 \div 8) - 2$

30

$(3 \times 6 \times 2) - (4 + 2)$

25

5^2

10

$(24 \div 6) \times 5 - 10$

One large office lit overnight wastes enough energy to drive a small car more than **200** miles.

$1800 \div 9$

Page 27

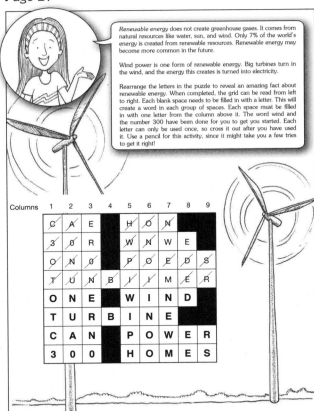

Renewable energy does not create greenhouse gases. It comes from natural resources like water, sun, and wind. Only 7% of the world's energy is created from renewable resources. Renewable energy may become more common in the future.

Wind power is one form of renewable energy. Big turbines turn in the wind, and the energy this creates is turned into electricity.

Rearrange the letters in the puzzle to reveal an amazing fact about renewable energy. When completed, the grid can be read from left to right. Each blank space needs to be filled in with a letter. This will create a word in each group of spaces. Each space must be filled in with one letter from the column above it. The word wind and the number 300 have been done for you to get you started. Each letter can only be used once, so cross it out after you have used it. Use a pencil for this activity, since it might take you a few tries to get it right!

Columns 1 2 3 4 5 6 7 8 9

C	A	E		H	O	N		
3	0	R		W	N	W	E	
O	N	0		P	E	D	S	
T	U	N	B	I	I	M	E	R
O	N	E		W	I	N	D	
T	U	R	B	I	N	E		
C	A	N		P	O	W	E	R
3	0	0		H	O	M	E	S

Page 28

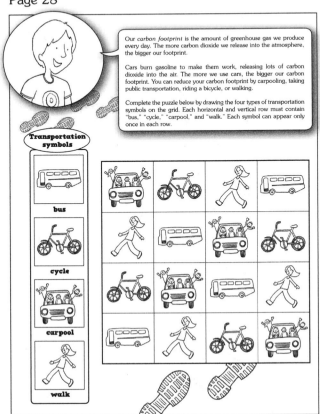

Our *carbon footprint* is the amount of greenhouse gas we produce every day. The more carbon dioxide we release into the atmosphere, the bigger our footprint.

Cars burn gasoline to make them work, releasing lots of carbon dioxide into the air. The more we use cars, the bigger our carbon footprint. You can reduce your carbon footprint by carpooling, taking public transportation, riding a bicycle, or walking.

Complete the puzzle below by drawing the four types of transportation symbols on the grid. Each horizontal and vertical row must contain "bus," "cycle," "carpool," and "walk." Each symbol can appear only once in each row.

Transportation symbols

bus

cycle

carpool

walk

Page 29

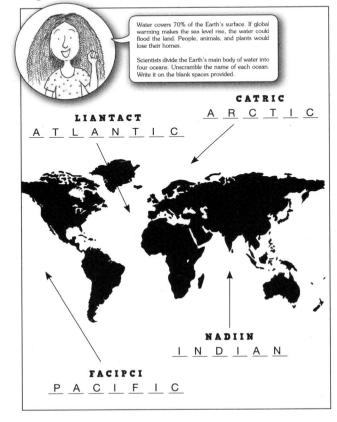

Water covers 70% of the Earth's surface. If global warming makes the sea level rise, the water could flood the land. People, animals, and plants would lose their homes.

Scientists divide the Earth's main body of water into four oceans. Unscramble the name of each ocean. Write it on the blank spaces provided.

CATRIC
A R C T I C

LIANTACT
A T L A N T I C

NADIIN
I N D I A N

FACIPCI
P A C I F I C

42

1) Windows are left open with the radiator on
2) Clothes are drying on the radiator when they could be drying outside in the sun
3) The lamp does not need to be on in the middle of the day
4) The computer is on but the boy isn't using it
5) The mobile phone is still plugged in even though it is fully charged
6) The tap has been left running
7) The electric heater is on even though it is a warm day
8) The main light does not need to be on in the middle of the day
9) The television has been left on even though the boy is not watching it
10) The stereo is on even though the boy is listening to music on his MP3 player

Team Recycle has a motto to help us remember to be good to the environment. Unscramble the letters on the sign to find out what it is.

CUREED
SEERU
CREYLEC

ANSWER:
R E D U C E, R E U S E, R E C Y C L E !

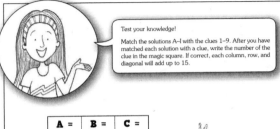

Test your knowledge!

Match the solutions A–I with the clues 1–9. After you have matched each solution with a clue, write the number of the clue in the magic square. If correct, each column, row, and diagonal will add up to 15.

A = 4	B = 9	C = 2
D = 3	E = 5	F = 7
G = 8	H = 1	I = 6

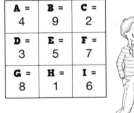

A Dendroclimatology   **D** The founder of Earth Day   **G** Methane
B Acid Rain   **E** Aluminum   **H** Ice Glaciers
C E-waste   **F** Fossil Fuels   **I** Carbon Dioxide

1) These may melt because of global warming
2) This is a term for electronic waste
3) Gaylord Nelson
4) Scientists study tree rings to find out about our climate. What term describes their job?
5) This form of waste takes 500 years to break down
6) Cars produce this greenhouse gas
7) Natural resources found in the ground which we burn to make energy
8) This gas is emitted from cows' waste
9) When chemicals mix with water in the air they can poison lakes and animals may die